Brenda!
So great to meet
you! Hope you
like the book!
♡ Kim

Kim Foster Carlson

Good Enough

How to overcome fear of failure and perfectionism to live your best life.

BALBOA
PRESS

A DIVISION OF HAY HOUSE

Balboa Press books may be ordered through booksellers or by contacting:

Balboa Press
A Division of Hay House
1663 Liberty Drive
Bloomington, IN 47403
www.balboapress.com
1 (877) 407-4847

Because of the dynamic nature of the Internet, any web addresses or links contained in this book may have changed since publication and may no longer be valid. The views expressed in this work are solely those of the author and do not necessarily reflect the views of the publisher, and the publisher hereby disclaims any responsibility for them.

The author of this book does not dispense medical advice or prescribe the use of any technique as a form of treatment for physical, emotional, or medical problems without the advice of a physician, either directly or indirectly. The intent of the author is only to offer information of a general nature to help you in your quest for emotional and spiritual well-being. In the event you use any of the information in this book for yourself, which is your constitutional right, the author and the publisher assume no responsibility for your actions.

Any people depicted in stock imagery provided by Thinkstock are models, and such images are being used for illustrative purposes only. Certain stock imagery © Thinkstock.

Print information available on the last page.

ISBN: 978-1-5043-9599-1 (sc)
ISBN: 978-1-5043-9601-1 (hc)
ISBN: 978-1-5043-9600-4 (e)

Library of Congress Control Number: 2018900982

Balboa Press rev. date: 01/24/2018

To my imperfectly perfect husband, Mike, who teaches me every day that love and laughter truly are the best medicine. And to my children, Kasey, Taylor, and Connor, who teach me every day what it means to be.

Contents

Introduction

Failure is so important. We speak about
success all the time. It is the ability to resist
failure or use failure that often leads to greater
success. I've met people who don't want to try
for fear of failing.

—J. K. Rowling

Many top major league baseball players fail 70 percent of the time. Batters with over a .300 average, which is considered very good, still strike out at least seven out of ten times they are up at bat. Professional basketball players are considered at the top of their game if they make 50 percent of their shots. That means that half of the time, they miss the hoop.

In the NFL, a professional quarterback who completes 60 percent of his passes is considered the most elite in the game.

That means 40 percent of the time, the quarterback fails at his job.

Failing is so integral to sport that it is woven into the success of any athlete. Wardell Stephen Curry, who brought the Golden State Warriors their first NBA championship in forty years, said it best:

"I'm not the guy who's afraid of failure. I like to take risks, take the big shot."

If you have seen Curry play, you've noticed that he likes to take the high-risk shot, sometimes from half-court, and he often makes it.

Curry's college coach at Davidson, a small Division 3 school, saw the no-fear quality in the star early on. "He had no fear of failure," Bob McKillop said. "If he missed a shot, missed five shots, he didn't care. It didn't disrupt him. It didn't destroy his focus. He knew he was going to make the next five."

Steph Curry uses failure to his advantage. When he had his worst shooting performance in the last two seasons in game two of the NBA finals, Curry and his coach talked only of not letting failure define him.

"I'm not going to let one game kind of alter my confidence," Curry said. "I know that as a team we're not going to let one game alter our belief that we're going to win the series. We've got to move on and be ready to play a good team that's ready to go home."

Curry's coach, Steve Kerr concurred.

"It happens to everybody, whether you're the MVP or a role player. Sometimes the shots don't go in. Steph will bounce back. He's a great player."

(*Sporting News*, Cory Collins, April 27, 2015)

(*New York Post*, Marc Berman, June 8, 2015)

Is Steph Curry perfect? No. But is he good enough? You bet.

I look forward to watching him fail with no fear for many years to come.

Tom Brady was drafted into the NFL after playing for the University of Michigan as a backup quarterback for his first two years. The New England Patriots picked Brady in the sixth round. He was the 199th pick in the 2000 NFL draft. Brady thought he would have gone in the first or second round, but he was passed over for six other quarterbacks. He started his first season with the Patriots as the fourth-string quarterback. By season's end, he was the number one backup. By the next year, he was the starter, and he is still playing at the age of forty. Five Super Bowl rings later and still those who know Brady say the same things about him: He is fearless, he is not afraid of failure, and he remains humble.

Tom Brady is good enough.

I struggled with trying to be perfect—a perfect athlete, wife, mother, and journalist. I was none of these. But I now welcome failure, not as the enemy, but as a roadmap to lead me to greater success. It hasn't been easy. I had to learn the hard way.

"You're human," my therapist said. "It's okay to make mistakes."

But from an early age, I was taught the exact opposite.

"I got my report card today," I remember telling my mother when I started middle school. "Six As and one B+. Look ..."

"Well," Mother said in her perfectionistic, judging, British nanny voice (she really is a former British nanny), "why wasn't that B+ an A?"

My mother was like Mary Poppins, very strict but very loving, and always pushing her children to do better. Those perfectionistic genes were honed early and continued through high school, as I excelled in the extremely competitive sport of swimming. My parents, both firstborn children, both highly driven, instilled in all of us to try our best and make good decisions, which for a budding perfectionist like myself meant making no mistakes. So it was no surprise that I chose a college major where you cannot make mistakes: journalism. In my first reporting class, the professor laid down the law. "If your story has no mistakes, typos, or any word misspelled, you will get an A," he said, peeking over his reading glasses as if to say, Go ahead and test me. "One mistake, and your paper will be returned to you with a big red F on the front."

No pressure there.

He did give his students the option of fixing mistakes and turning the paper back in for a lower grade, but I wasn't having any of that.

Telling perfectionists that they have to be perfect is like giving them their drug of choice. And I performed well under pressure. But when there was no pressure, there was no performing for me. That is when another "P" word entered my life: procrastination. Perfection and procrastination go together like "peas and carrots," quoting Forrest Gump.

By the time I graduated, I had perfected procrastination to an art form and left Cal Poly with an unfinished senior project that I finally finished a few years later. Well, seven years later.

I decided on a career in radio, a career where if you mispronounce a word, stumble on a phrase, or forget your traffic anchor's name, you get called in to the principal's office, otherwise known as the news director. The by-product of perfectionism and procrastination—anxiety—became my constant companion. I was nervous about whether the equipment was going to work on the air. I worried about how my voice sounded on the air. I was anxious about whether I was fair and accurate in my storytelling. And what about my coworkers—did they think I was a good journalist? The list went on and on.

I remember sitting with the news director who hired me to do sports back in 1993.

"You know, Kim," he said, "you're a woman. And as a female sports anchor, you're going to be held to a higher standard than the men. If you mispronounce a team, athlete, or coach, you'll lose all credibility. So don't do it. Ever."

Consequently, I spent every free moment watching sports, learning the names of every major league baseball, basketball, and football player.

Just when my anxiety was reaching new heights, it became clear that my third child, Connor, was not meeting his developmental milestones. He was a late walker and a very late talker. In time, the word that no parent wants to hear—autism—was discussed as a possible diagnosis.

I went from doctor to doctor, trying to find one who would say that my son didn't have a neurological disability. But then one day, a developmental pediatrician told me point-blank, "Connor has autism. It's a serious disability marked by lack of language and social skills. He will probably never drive a car or get married, and you better just accept it."

That will be $500, please, and don't let the door hit you on the way out. That was my introduction to the world of disability. Driving a car and getting married are two major milestones every parent wants to see his or her child achieve. The possibility those weren't going to happen threw me into the most perfectionistic anxiety-driven tornado; by the time the twister had left the building, I was sitting in the therapist's chair, utterly exhausted and depressed.

I found myself on the couch of Dr. Mary Spencer, my therapist, like someone hanging onto the end of a long, fraying rope. Everyone had told me I needed help, but I thought I could manage on my own.

What? Me? I'm perfect. What's your problem?

By the time I went to see Mary, I had been in a downward

spiral for a long time, and it took even longer until I could climb out and see the sun again.

"Anger is really all about fear, not being in control, things not being perfect," I told Mary, a charmingly calm woman dressed in long flowing clothes with matching shoes. When she told me it was okay that I wasn't perfect, I went on the defensive. What did she know?

But in reality, my life was far from perfect. Despite hours and hours of speech and behavioral therapy, Connor showed little improvement by age seven. I was so preoccupied with his care that my career as a radio news anchor was floundering. And with my anger at the world, I was not a very nice person to be around. *What's the cure?* I thought to myself as I sunk into Mary's green velvet couch, with a box of tissues next to me. I hoped that she could just give me a pill that would make me happy again.

But no such luck. She gave me homework for the next week.

"You have to go through this week," she said, "not thinking everything is either perfect or a failure. You have to think of things as good enough."

"What am I supposed to do, not try?" I asked.

"No, just let yourself off the hook. Think, what you've done for that day is good enough."

I'll play your game, therapist lady, I thought, *but it is not going to work. No one wants good enough.*

But in truth, I had become so fearful of doing the wrong thing that I became frozen, paralyzed, unable to make decisions and live a productive life. Those two words, "good enough," changed my thoughts and eventually changed my life.

In this book, I'm going to tell you how I did it.

If I can do it, so can you.

Like every one of you, I am still a work in progress. I don't have all the answers. But I have learned some valuable lessons that have helped me live a life that is good enough.

Chapter 1

The "P" Word ────────

We live in a society that celebrates being perfect—from beauty to brains. We all know someone who in our minds is the ideal person: the person in school who had all the friends, the friend who can whip up a gourmet meal with ingredients found in the refrigerator. In an ideal world, we would like to be happy with ourselves, but in the real world, we don't feel we are good enough. The best solution to becoming the best version of you—with all your foibles and quirks—is to embrace your imperfections.

This doesn't give you permission to become a sloth and do nothing. But how great would it be to embrace your flaws—love the parts of you that you once thought of as your shortcomings—and see them as uniquely you?

Perfectionism keeps you from your true expression and creativity as well. It invites fear and doubt. Being flawless doesn't help fill you up. Being real and being flawed invites real connections to others. So what can you do to combat a bad case of the perfection?

You can see mistakes as information that you must have to become successful. Learn something from them that you can improve on. Don't be proud of being perfect. Don't confuse perfection with high standards. Healthy standards are better. Practice being imperfect. Take a day to do everything imperfectly. Mistakes mean progress.

Apple founder Steve Jobs probably had a few bad versions of a cell phone before he and his team invented the iPhone.

Be kind to yourself. Perfectionists are critical of themselves and others. Be perfectly imperfect with being yourself.

Chapter 2

Problems Are a Good Thing

In his 2016 book *The Subtle Art of Not Giving a F**K*, Mark Manson's counterintuitive approach preaches that life is essentially an endless series of problems. The solution to one problem is merely the creation of another. Instead of asking, "How can I get rid of my problems?" the question should be "What are the problems that excite me? What are the problems I am willing to sacrifice for, to work for?"

Manson offers an example of wanting to get in shape:

You can solve this problem by buying a gym membership, which gives you a set of new problems: finding time in your day to go to the gym and budgeting the extra expense. Both are not bad problems to have but are problems, nonetheless. And that is the key to Manson's mantra: Find problems that you are interested in solving. Here is where perfection comes into play. If a problem arises, you have two choices: decide on a solution or distract yourself from the problem.

Distractions are a perfectionist's best friend. They can help you to pretend that the problem is not really there. What are your favorite distractions: watching television, playing video games, getting high?

Deciding on a solution seems like the much better way to go. Solutions are active decisions to move you forward. Distractions keep you right where you are: miserable. The key here is to honestly identify the problem and the distraction.

If you have a job, for example, where you work long hours with a horrible boss who ignores you, promotes everyone but you, and basically makes your life miserable, you have a few choices: find a new job, live with the fact that you are not appreciated, or confront your boss.

If you are not looking at solutions, then you are probably distracting yourself with things such as watching way too much Netflix, eating way too much junk food, and sitting on the couch for days, weeks, months, years.

What a waste.

So what can you do? Make a list of solutions to your problem. Make a list of your distractions, and be honest.

Which list looks better?

I did this myself for a similar boss problem and can tell you it works. But it's not as easy as it looks. Many of my distractions had become habits that were difficult to break, but they needed to be broken.

Not sure you're ready? Ask for help. Some people are afraid of therapy. My sister, who is a therapist, told me it's the mentally healthy people who come to therapy; the unstable ones think that everyone else is the problem. Support groups are always an option; they can be truly supportive and not just a place for everyone to complain about their families and each other. A compassionate friend can also be a great place to start. The more problems you solve, the easier it will get to work out the next problem that is just around the corner. Limiting the distractions are key, so put down that piece of cake, turn off the Netflix, and start writing those lists. Once you are on the problem/solution gravy train, the next stop is happiness. Happiness, according to Manson, occurs by solving problems. It's an activity.

Completing a marathon makes you happier than eating a chocolate cake. Raising a child makes you happier than beating a video game. Starting a small business with friends and struggling to make money makes you happier than buying a new computer.

The road to these goals can be paved with potholes, pitfalls, and perfectionistic procrastination. But once you get to the finish line, you realize that, in fact, it was the journey that brought you the most happiness of all.

Chapter 3

Too Blessed to Be Stressed ▬

"I'm just blessed to play this game," you often hear from professional athletes. "I'm just thankful for all the blessings in my life." In reality, what these athletes are practicing is gratitude. And gratitude is the stepping-stone to happiness. But how do you count your blessings when you feel lonely, anxious, and stressed about work, family, friends, and money?

Research shows that those who practice gratitude are happier. Gratitude helps you stay in the present moment, interrupting your negative thoughts about the past or future.

Just like everything else, you have the choice in any situation to choose gratitude. When your parents are being crazy and overbearing, you can be grateful that they are still around and care enough to smother you, in a good way. When you are single and ready to mingle but no one seems to be available, be grateful you live in a time where all you need is a cell phone and a few apps to meet and greet a wide variety of people.

Part of practicing gratitude is seeing the glass as half-full, but it's more than that. It's being thankful that there is even a glass, no matter how full or empty. Your mind naturally goes first to the negative. I'll never fill that glass, for a number of reasons. This way of thinking has kept us from dying out as a species, but it's more powerful than feeling joy. That's the reason you need to override these negative thoughts with thankful ones. But it takes practice and lots of practice.

Luckily, you can learn this at any age and change your life for the better.

So how do you learn the practice of gratitude? Simple. Wake up every day, and before you brush your teeth, think of three things you are grateful for in your life. Then think of someone you want to thank for something they helped you with. Do this for four weeks and see how you feel. My guess is you will feel a lot better about people and about your life.

You can start with something little, like thanking the person on social media. If you are having trouble thinking of three things to be grateful for, think small. Maybe you are thankful that there was enough milk for your cereal this morning. Maybe you are grateful that your new puppy finally pooped outside and not on the floor. Maybe you are just happy you woke up and got dressed.

Chapter 4

Relaxed Confidence

Football coach Pete Carroll coined the phrase "relaxed confidence" and preached it to his players. When your mind is quiet, according to Carroll, and without fear, you perform better. Carroll implements meditation and yoga into his players' daily routine. No one is required to go, but many players say it has made all the difference in their game. Carroll's research, along with psychologist Michael Gervais, shows that happy football players make better players. Players undergo brain performance testing to better understand how they deal with stress. All of the players, coaches, and staff implement a positive mind-set. Yelling and foul language are not allowed, making for a kinder and gentler organization—and a winning one as well.

No one embraces Carroll's mantra more than his Seahawk quarterback, Russell Wilson. Wilson has meetings with

Gervais, where they work on techniques like visualization, which involves seeing yourself in winning situations. They work on staying in the present and quieting the mind. Carroll also believes in simulating games in practice, so by the time the players get to the game, they are playing with relaxed confidence.

It's no wonder many other coaches have picked up on Carroll's techniques, including Steve Kerr, coach of the Golden State Warriors.

Kerr has said that 80 percent of coaching is in the atmosphere you create the relationships between the players. Kerr headed up to Seattle to take in a Seahawks' practice. What he saw and then implemented for his team included playing music during practice. Both Carroll and Kerr celebrate their players' individuality, while at the same time preaching a team mentality. Being relaxed but competitive and confident. This type of mentality can be translated into anything you want to accomplish and can definitely help keep those perfectionistic tendencies from creeping up and ruining an imperfectly perfect performance. From speaking in public, to performing a play, to swimming a race, staying in the moment in relaxed confidence will not only help you do better, you will enjoy the journey more.

In his book *Win Forever,* Carroll talks about competition not against others, but against yourself in every area of your life. When we are confident, we become focused and almost move in slower motion, and that's the state he wants his players to be in during a game. He also wants to keep things light and fun. The Seahawks often play other sports in preseason and during the season and even have a basketball hoop at their training site for shooting competitions in the middle of meetings. [1]

---

[1]   Pete Carroll, Kristoffer A. Garin, and Yogi Roth. *Winning Forever*, Portfolio Trade NY, 2011.

Chapter 5

It's Not about You

Part of the perfection myth is believing that everyone is watching you and judging you, so if you appear perfect, no one can criticize you. In reality, not everyone is going to like you, not matter what you do. People come with their hidden biases about everything, including how you look. Whether it's your clothes, your hair, or the way you say the word "cheese," someone is not going to like you, and that's okay. The only people you need to worry about are those who are in the arena with you. Winston Churchill's quote resonates well in almost any situation where you are being judged:

> It is not the critic who counts; not the man who points out how the strong man stumbles, or where the doer of deeds could have done them better. The credit belongs to the man who is

actually in the arena, whose face is marred by dust and sweat and blood; who strives valiantly; who errs, who comes short again and again, because there is no effort without error and shortcoming; but who does actually strive to do the deeds; who knows great enthusiasms, the great devotions; who spends himself in a worthy cause; who at the best knows in the end the triumph of high achievement, and who at the worst, if he fails, at least fails while daring greatly, so that his place shall never be with those cold and timid souls who neither know victory nor defeat.[2]

-Theodore Roosevelt

How many people are in your arena? Aside from your family and a few close friends or colleagues, whose opinion really matters? When people are critical toward you, it really doesn't have much to do with you. It has a lot more to do with them. When you don't succeed, it doesn't mean you are an unsuccessful person; it means you tried and were unsuccessful in your attempt. And you will continue to fail at many things, over and over. The hope is that you learn from your mistakes and use them to make new and better mistakes.

---

[2]   The Man In The Arena" Speech at the Sorbonne Paris, France April 23, 1910

It is easier said than done to not care what people think, but it will make your life much more enjoyable. This doesn't mean you walk around being rude to everyone or being indifferent about important things in your life. That's just being lazy. It's deciding what is worthy of your time and attention. When you are younger, you have more energy to do more things and care more about a lot of things. As you age, you care less about the trivial things that don't matter and instead care more about the things that are meaningful in your life and let go of those opinions of people who at one time mattered but don't seem to anymore. [3]

-Brené Brown

---

[3] Brené Brown *Daring Greatly,* Avery NY 2012

Chapter 6

It's Okay to Be Average

I am a swimmer. Put me in the water, and I can do almost anything. On land, not so much. After college swimming was over, my triathlon friends talked me into doing a relay. All I would have to do is the swim. Sounds easy enough. And it was. Then I got the crazy idea that I can bike and run as well and should try my hand at a whole triathlon: swim-bike-run. Of course, I was fantastic at the swim which allowed me to be out way ahead of everyone else. If the bike ride had no hills, I was pretty good at that leg of the race. When it came to the running portion, boy, did I suck. Everyone passed me ... even my husband, who was a crappy swimmer but raced bikes and ran track. I ended up in the middle. Dare I say average? And happily, that was okay with this reformed perfectionist.

We all are good at some things and not so good (okay, really bad) at other things. And that's okay. Not everyone who paints is a Picasso, and not everyone who shoots three-pointers is Steph Curry. And if you ask Steph how many hours he has put into his craft, he may say not enough, but he definitely has dedicated all his energy to becoming the best in the world. For every Steph Curry, there are five million basketball players not hitting a record number of threes.

Many people who become extraordinary at something are obsessed with improvement and will continue working long after many others have quit and gone home. If you want to be better than anyone else all the time, that will just set you up for failure. Mark Manson is right on the money when he writes, "There are over 7.2 billion people on this planet, and really only about a thousand of those have major worldwide influence at any given time. That leaves the other 7,199,999,000 +/- of us to come to terms with the limited scope of our lives." You can be strong in some areas and weak in others. If you excel at math or science, you are ahead of the curve in many areas of academics.

My son Connor is a truly gifted painter but has autism, and his language was delayed. I am a proven slug on land. It is those who spend hours and hours at the gym or in the pool perfecting their craft who have the best chance of being above average. It's the effort given that is the reward, not the outcome.

In the end, it comes down to appreciating the little things that you experience along the journey: the sunset you see at the end of the day with your spouse, the long talk with an old friend, or the great dinner out with your kids. Those things are pretty average in the scheme of life but will mean the most to you in the long run.

Chapter 7

90 Percent

S wimmers have a workout set called "threshold." It means how long can you go at 80 to 90 percent, with the hope of going the distance of the race. Pacing yourself is key to this set. If you go out too hard and, say, give 95 or 100 percent, you will burn out and "blow up," as they say, and barely finish the race. This threshold theory can be applied to life and to the all-or-nothing thinking of perfectionists.

Those who are afraid of making mistakes become so paralyzed that they end up not starting projects or not finishing something they need to get done.

One way to trick your brain to not go into panic mode is to say to yourself, *I'm going to give it 90 percent effort.* That doesn't mean you are slacking off or not trying. Train your brain to understand that the effort of 90 percent is good enough to get the project completed. By using this thinking, you get yourself out of the all-or-nothing loop playing in your head. That is not easy to do at first, but this less-than-perfect work will actually give you more satisfaction than if you keep trying for perfection and never finish the work. With this 90 percent state of mind, you will keep higher standards and perform better work over time than you would have done in your perfectionist state.

Sometimes, the problem is getting started toward the 90 percent. As with anything, starting is the hardest part. I went through it with writing this book. One of the best solutions I found was to not think but to act. I needed to just start writing, and as I continued to just write, the right thoughts about how I wanted the book to unfold became clear.

Many people wait to get motivated to write, or create, or even to get up off the couch, kind of like the chicken-before-the-egg concept. You have to take action, any action, and then the motivation to do more will emerge over time. You are more focused on getting started and less focused on failing in the attempt. The standards have been lowered—to about 90 percent. Voila.

So get off that couch and do something. Anything.

Sometimes, when your back is against the wall or you are in the last leg of a race, you can kick it into overdrive for the moment. But remaining in overdrive will wear you out and make you less productive in the long run. Athletes who overtrain by pushing their bodies past the breaking point, for example, often end up injured.

You need to know when to step on the gas and when to slow down. Successful athletes make a practice of watching for the warning signs from their bodies and adjust their workouts to help with rest and recovery.

This philosophy is the reason why New England Patriots quarterback Tom Brady is still going strong although he's forty years of age. Brady's schedule consists of treatment, workouts, food, recovery, practice, and rest. He says he is in better shape now than when he was drafted at twenty-three. When asked how long he wants to continue to play football, Brady says, "Forever."

Chapter 8

Moment by Moment ▬▬▬▬▬

In his book, *The Power of Now*, Eckhart Tolle explains how worry and fear stem from not living in the present moment. If you constantly look to the past or worry about what will happen in the future, you are taken away from the now.

"Above all, the only thing you have to heal is the present thought," Tolle writes. "Get that right and the whole picture will change into one of harmony and joy."

Tolle believes that your ego takes you out of present moment and puts you into a sort of perfectionist whirlwind of wanting or needing more from a situation or person. By staying in the present moment, you stop those thoughts, many of them negative, from taking over. Tolle believes that much of your thinking is mindless and not needed and even interferes with having a great life. Some call it your inner bully or nasty roommate: the voice in your head that keeps you from becoming your best self. By asking yourself, *Am I having a problem right this second?* or *How am I feeling in this very moment?* you take yourself out of the catastrophizing thoughts of the past and future and just keep yourself in the now. If you suffer from anxiety at all, these insights from Tolle will change the way you think and therefore change your life.

These insights changed my life. In the depths of depression over Connor's autism, and with the help of my therapist, I practiced Tolle's philosophy and found that it was the only thing that really helped keep that anxiety from taking over:

- Don't seek happiness. If you seek it, you won't find it, because seeking is the antithesis of happiness. Happiness is ever elusive, but freedom from unhappiness is attainable now, by facing what is rather than making up stories about it.
- The primary cause of unhappiness is never the situation but your thoughts about it. Be aware of the thoughts you are thinking. Separate them from the situation, which is always neutral, which always is as it is.
- See if you can catch the voice in your head, perhaps in the very moment it complains about something, and recognize it for what it is: the voice of the ego, no more than a thought.

- Why do anxiety, stress, or negativity arise? Because you turned away from the present moment. And why did you do that? You thought something else was more important. One small error, one misperception, creates a world of suffering.

- People believe themselves to be dependent on what happens for their happiness. They don't realize that what happens is the most unstable thing in the universe. It changes constantly.

- Accept the present moment and find the perfection that is untouched by time.

- You don't become good by trying to be good, but by finding the goodness that is already within you and allowing that goodness to emerge.

- If peace is really what you want, then you will choose peace.

The only way to practice being in the moment is with meditation. I must admit that I am not very good at sitting still and being still. But once I was able to quiet my very active and talkative mind, I felt worry and anxiety leave my body; they were replaced with calm and peace. As little as five minutes a day of practicing meditation can do wonders for your mind and your mood. Let me give you a CliffsNotes version of how to meditate from Jack Kornfield's book *Meditation for Beginners*:

1. Find a quiet place where you won't be disturbed. To get started, it doesn't matter whether you sit or lay down, as long as you are comfortable. You can sit cross-legged, on the floor, or on a chair. If you can sit erect, then great. If not, it's just important to have your body in a somewhat stable position. Then have the palms of your hands face the sky.

2. Become present.

3. Become totally aware of your current surroundings. What do you hear? How does it feel to sit? Do you feel tension? Where are your thoughts?

4. Focus on your breath. As you take long and deep breaths, feel your breath move from your lungs and out through your nostrils or your throat. (Breathing through your nostrils is better, though either will work.) Your mind will wander (which is okay); just try your best to be as focused as possible.

5. Feel your body. Once you're focused, take notice of your body and assess how each body part feels. Start with the toes and work your way up to your head. If your mind continues to wander, then bring your thoughts back to your breath. Breathe five to ten times

with full concentration on each breath. Take it a step further and hum, "Om," as you breathe out.

Like anything, practice makes perfect. Make sure to carve out a time each and every day to practice.

Chapter 9

Me, Myself, and I ━━━━━━━━

M y friend and I used to marvel at the moms in the carpool
line, talking about their latest kitchen remodel or about
which fancy drapes they should buy for their living room. We
were both in the world of autism, wondering how we could
afford all those services the school district wouldn't pay for.
We couldn't help but compare our lives to theirs. The other
moms weren't having meetings with the teacher about how
far behind their child was. They weren't watching other kids
go off to a birthday party when their child wasn't invited.

What we didn't realize is that those moms had problems of
their own.

No one is perfect, and that's okay. In fact, that's great. If
you can accept yourself, warts and all, you'll be ahead of
the game when it comes to living your best life. If you know
you're not a high energy positive person all the time and have

to take breaks from being in a crowd, you will be a better friend, parent, and partner if you're able to be present in those moments where you are a little uncomfortable, knowing you will be getting a break down the road.

Life is not always easy; in fact, sometimes, it downright sucks. It's hard at those times to believe that anyone else is going through the same thing, but in reality, you are not alone. There are those who have experienced the same thing, whether it be losing a job, a parent, a child, or a marriage, and it's those who've had similar experiences that you need to reach out to for help. It's when you separate yourself from others, or compare yourself to someone that you start to go down the road to self-hatred and sabotage. You may compare yourself to those you perceive as more successful, whether it be their career, car, house, kids, or even how many likes they get on social media. Instead of putting these people on a pedestal, see them as humans with flaws, just like everyone else.

For example, your neighbor may have a Mercedes in the front driveway and an immaculate yard. But perhaps they have gone through a painful divorce or have health problems. Keep in mind that everyone goes through something at one time or another; this will make you more compassionate, and it will make you realize that you're okay and I'm okay.

I'm sure you are familiar with that person at work, on your sports team, or even in your family. The narcissist. Narcissists are self-centered, so absorbed in their own life that they don't even realize there is anyone else who matters besides themselves. These emotional vampires can suck the joy right out of a room.

Best to steer clear of them, or when you have to interact, keep it brief and don't try to engage in an argumentative conversation. Narcissists lack empathy and aren't able to feel what another person is going through. It's simply not in their DNA. This is where perfectionism can rear its ugly head yet again. Trying to live up to a narcissistic person's expectations can be exhausting, especially if the person is a parent. Narcissistic parents believe that their child is extension of them. They believe that everything that is happening to the child is happening to them as well. The good, the bad, and the ugly. "Helicopter" parenting is an extension of this, as parents live vicariously through their children's lives. Parents who have this tendency can go a long way by allowing their children to make mistakes, often, and without harsh criticism, and to encourage them to be good enough.

Chapter 10

If You're Not First, You're Last

We celebrate winners. We are disappointed when we lose. Just take a look at professional sports—the Super Bowl, the NBA championships, the World Series are just a few of the events that celebrate the winner and demonize the loser. But what about the losing team? After the game, many of the players and coaches say they're grateful they made it that far and hope to be back next year, with a different result. In that moment, they played the best they could, and that's all you can ask. Sometimes it's not first place that is good enough, but third place.

That is exactly what happened to my daughter in the summer of 2009. Kasey had qualified first for the finals at the World Championship Trials in the hundred-meter breaststroke. The top two places advanced to the worlds in Rome. No one was giving her a chance that evening to make it onto the team.

At seventeen and the youngest in the final, her chances were good but not great, as the Olympian Rebecca Soni was also in the race. But they take only two swimmers, so she just had to be good enough that night. And she was. She finished second to Soni, earning a trip to Italy.

Once at the meet, Kasey was just happy to be at the party. She was already practicing gratitude and staying in the moment as she enjoyed being one of the youngest on the team and hanging out with swimming's elite. In the prelims, she finished eighth—just good enough to make the final. She was in lane eight for the final, and when they all came into the wall at the finish, Rebecca Soni was first, a Russian swimmer was second, and who was third, all the way over in lane eight?

Kasey.

She called me right away, and I heard such joy in her voice as she told me she had never been so happy in her life to get third place. That's because only the top three, just like at the Olympics, get a medal. Now swimming is an up-and-down sport, and not all of her moments went exactly like in Rome, but it gave her the confidence and the insight into her swimming career that she doesn't have to be perfect, just good enough.

Kasey was one of those athletes who could do any sport and

be good at it. She excelled at swimming, along with her sister, Taylor, and so both girls went into year-round swimming at an early age. Now as adults, they ask why I didn't put them in volleyball, as they are both over six feet tall. Kasey won junior nationals by the time she was fourteen and spent the next three years on the USA National Junior team. She traveled quite a bit and still has friends today that she met during that time. Taylor also excelled but at a little slower pace; she earned a scholarship to UCLA and made the NCAA championships on the relay team. She looks back fondly on her years swimming in Los Angeles. Kasey's road was a little more up and down, with good years at the NCAAs and not-so-good years at other competitions. In the end, Kasey finished as an eighteen-time All-American and runner-up twice in events she didn't normally swim in high school. She was on the USA National team but didn't train intensively for the Olympic trials because of the college season. She retired with no regrets.

She felt she was good enough.

Did she want to be an Olympian? Sure, who wouldn't? But only two swimmers earn a spot in each event, every four years. Kasey realized that she wasn't going to base her entire success on one swim meet. I was very proud of her for realizing this because many of her teammates did not and struggled with what they thought they could have achieved during their swimming careers. Swimming taught my daughters so much more than just looking at a black line at the bottom of the pool. It taught them to fail, a lot and early on, and to keep going. It taught them to schedule their time, and to work hard and see results. It taught them how to be good enough.

Chapter 11

Can't Get You Out of My Head ▪

My inner critic is pretty strong. Of course, it has a British voice and sounds like my mom, but that's probably because she was a perfectionist herself and tried her best to impose her crazy perfectionism on us. After coming to my house for a visit, she'd find twelve things I should immediately fix. She often rearranged my cabinets, making it difficult to find things that she felt were in a better place. There was a right way and a wrong way, and I always seemed to be doing things incorrectly, in her mind.

Perfection problems arise when your inner critic, the bully voice inside your head, fills you with self-doubt and self-sabotage. It says you should be doing this or you can't possibly think you can do that. The voice tells you all of the bad things people have told you over the years: teachers, parents, relatives, and even friends.

The result is that you crave approval from others in hopes of stopping the inner critic. This voice stops you from trying new things, for fear of making a mistake. It constantly compares you to other people instead of letting you see the good in everyone.

So how can you stop these automatic critical thoughts and replace them with kind, loving thoughts? It's not as easy as it might seem, especially if that inner critic has a stronghold on your psyche. The best way that I have found to combat these thoughts is with a test developed by author Byron Katie. It is called "The Work" and it consists of asking yourself four questions:

1) Is the thought true?
2) Can you absolutely know it's true?
3) What happens when you believe this thought?
4) Who would you be without this thought?

A good example of using the Work:

"They're not open to my ideas."

Is it true? (Answer only yes or no; if no, go to #3) Is it true that they are not open to anything new? Be still. Wait for the heart's response.

Can you absolutely know that it's true? (Yes or no) Can you

absolutely know that they have no openness at all? Can you absolutely know how they truly feel inside?

How do you react, what happens, when you believe that thought? "They're not open to my ideas." Do you experience anger, stress, or disappointment? How do you treat them? How do these reactions feel? How do you treat yourself? Does this thought bring stress or peace into your life? Be still; notice how you react when you think this.

Who would you be without the thought? Close your eyes. Take a slow, deep breath. Picture yourself in their presence, in that situation. Now imagine looking at them, just for a moment, without the thought, *They are not open to my ideas*. What do you see? What would your work/life look like without that thought?

After answering the four questions, then you do the turnaround: "They are open to my ideas." Or "I'm not open to myself." Our thoughts, especially the automatic ones, are not often good for us. Using the Work will help you to get out of those thoughts and through the perfection anxiety loop very quickly. [4]

---

[4]   *Loving What Is* Byron Katie, Harmony Books, NY 2002

Chapter 12

The Small Stuff ————————

I hate to admit it, but I often let my kids fail. I told them that I would bring them their band instruments to school the first time they forgot them, but after that, they were on their own. It would mean a lower grade, but that's probably the only way they would learn. I could spend every week driving up to the school and dropping off their flute or trombone or anything else they forgot, but I didn't want to be that mom. I often acted like I didn't have a clue so that they would get a clue. I told my kids I could do their laundry, but I've been known to turn everything red, so they decided they were better off doing their laundry themselves. I know it wasn't the best parenting, but I was terrified they would grow up like I did and not know how to be independent. I wanted them to make mistakes and survive.

I sometimes brought them food for their lunch break, but that was for a selfish reason: I missed them during the school day and wanted to see them.

Perfectionists worry about every little detail, even those that are insignificant in the big picture of life. They agonize over the exact wording in an email or worry about what restaurant to go to or what movie to download. Small stuff can overwhelm and paralyze a perfectionist. A way to combat this behavior is to ask yourself these questions: Does this really matter? If so, will it matter in a few days, weeks, months, years from now? What is the worst-case scenario? If that is the worst case, will I survive?

The best way to survive the small stuff is to make small mistakes on purpose. Yes, that means deliberately doing something you feel is going to drive the perfectionist in you insane. How about walking around with a stain on your shirt, or being late to a lunch, or leaving your house messy when you know someone is coming over? I know it's crazy, but it actually works. It's like when someone who's afraid of flying forces himself to get on an airplane.

You just need to mess up your hair a little, as scary as that may sound.

If you are still having trouble over the small stuff, try this: Give yourself a time limit, say ten minutes, and write down all your little worries, fears, and anxieties. When time is up, take the piece of paper, crumble it up, and throw it in the trash. Then give yourself permission to not worry about those little things anymore.

Sweating about everything can have negative consequences to your physical health, as well.

A recent study out of Oregon State University found that older men who obsess over every little annoyance lived shorter lives than those who let things roll off their backs. "It's not the number of hassles that does you in; it's the perception of them being a big deal that causes problems," Carolyn Aldwin, the director of the Center for Healthy Aging Research at OSU, said in the study. "Taking things in stride may protect you."

Once again, that doesn't mean that you go around in life without a care in the world. Those people usually don't get much done in life. [5]

---

[5]   Lindsay Holmes. "How to Stop Sweating the Small Stuff." http://www.huffingtonpost.com/2014/09/12/sweating-the-small-stuff_n_5804524.html)

Chapter 13

The Twenty-Four-Hour Cleanse

Don't worry. It's not what you think. No weird green juices are involved in this cleanse. This cleanse rids your brain of those automatic negative thoughts that take over and make you miserable. Those thoughts make your perfectionistic tendencies go into overdrive and make you feel like you are not good enough.

The first step in the twenty-four-hour cleanse is to get yourself into a relaxed state by sitting in quiet place and doing some deep breathing. Then, as you relax, start to recognize the automatic thoughts that come into your mind. My mind would probably go to all the things I need to get done that day and what a waste of time it is to do this exercise. As soon as you notice these thoughts, say to yourself, *I'm going to like whatever thoughts come into my mind. Whatever my thoughts are, I'm going to be at peace with, including the negative thoughts.*

This is hard to do at first, but with practice, these new likable thoughts will become automatic. Once you feel like you have a good grasp of being with your likable thoughts, then try to go twenty-four hours, one day, with these thoughts and see how your view of the world changes. When you take a negative thought, such as, *I hate my job*, and have the feeling of enjoying that thought, the two feelings cannot coexist. And since you are choosing the loving feeling, the negative thought just disappears. This involves some heavy brain lifting, because just repeating positive thoughts or affirmations is not going to cut it. You have to have the positive feeling along with it. What if you can't muster up liking your negative thought?

Another quick way to turn things around is to try and think of one of the happiest times in your life. It could be a graduation, a marriage, or an award. Visualize yourself at that moment and feel what it was like: the smells, the sounds, and the real feelings of happiness and joy. It's hard to stay in a negative space when you do this exercise.

When you experience these happy and joyous emotions, your brain wants to experience more of them and looks to open up more options for you to continue to feel this way. The opposite is true for negative emotions. They tend to close you off and limit your higher thinking, otherwise known as the reptilian brain. It's your survival instinct kicking in. But you don't live in the wild anymore. This type of brain activity comes up often, though, in modern society, in the form of stress. When you find yourself stressed out with all the things you need to get done in one day, this might send your brain into survival mode and you to the couch, overwhelmed and paralyzed, unable to complete the list. Sound familiar?

Procrastination is perfection's ugly stepsister. Putting things off because you don't have the time or energy right now is different from the all-or-nothing attitude of perfection. If it's not going to be perfect, then it's not worth even trying. Calming down that reptilian brain and replacing it with positive thoughts and feelings will go a long way to getting you off the couch and ready to tackle the world … and your to-do list.

Chapter 14

Here Comes the Judge ━━━━━

Okay. This is a hard one.

As a journalist, I am constantly judging people, stories, and ideas to get to the facts. And the fact is, I can be quite critical of myself and others in my job, and that, in turn, can make me quite critical in my personal life. Hence, my problem with perfection: No one could live up to my ridiculous standards, especially not myself. But when you judge yourself and others, you are really judging yourself. For example, have you ever yelled at someone who cut you off while driving? Put yourself in the other person's shoes for a moment. When someone is annoying you, they may in fact have poor social skills or even a hidden disability. If someone is standing too close or invading your personal space, they may not even realize they are doing it. I have to admit that before I had a child with special needs, I was guilty of judging parents whose kids were misbehaving, crying, or just behaving like toddlers. Once I had a child with autism, people judged me whenever my child wouldn't sit, wouldn't eat, or was a downright pain anywhere and everywhere we went. If there was a public place to throw a tantrum, Connor would find it. I now try not to judge when I see a child having a hard time; instead, I try to have sympathy for the parents and siblings. If you see a child having a hard time, don't judge; instead, understand, help if you can, and tell those who are judging to shut up.

Most people don't go through their day thinking about how to be really annoying. They are just living their lives. I see this quite a bit with Connor. He stands too close to people at the grocery checkout line. He often doesn't look people in the eye when speaking with them. Some people totally get that he has autism and realize he isn't trying to irritate them. Others are just annoyed at him for invading their space. Some just point and stare or make rude comments. Once again, you have to go back to the "people in your arena" mantra. Those who have been through the gauntlet with you and understand your path are the only ones whose opinions you should care about, not some random person at the grocery store.

One of the best ways to get out of that critical view of life is to feel good about yourself. As author Brené Brown writes in her book *Daring Greatly*, "If I feel good about my parenting,

I have no interest in judging other people's choices. If I feel good about my body, I don't go around making fun of other people's weight or appearance. We're hard on each other because were using each other as a launching pad out of our own perceived deficiency."

It may take some reframing on your part to get out of judging others. What if that person is just doing something differently than you would it?

That person may have an alternate way to solve a problem that you didn't think of. Maybe it didn't work for you when you tried it; that doesn't mean it's wrong. It's just another way of looking at the problem. Some solutions are not easy to recognize, especially in the heat of the moment. But the more open-minded you can be, the less critical you become. And in the end, you are more like other people than different from them. And in the end, you and I both make mistakes, but that's okay. We are good enough.

Chapter 15

It's Everything

When I am on the radio, people tend to have the same comments. "You are actually *on* the radio?" is one of my favorites. "Do you write your own stories?" is another good one. Why people want to know that is beyond me. Sometimes, I have a writer and producer; other times, I write my own stories. When I do sports on the radio, the critics come out from all corners of the room. "*You* do sports?" like it is offensive that a woman actually knows what a pass route is or a five-three defense. I used to get so offended and often took everything personally. Once again, having a child with special needs changed all that. I learned some people are truly clueless; a lot of them have absolutely no idea what you go through with a child with autism. Those people are just ignorant about what your life is like. "You should teach your son to stop staring," people will say, or "Why don't you leave him at home when you go to the grocery store?"

I've learned to let a lot of that stuff to roll of my back, but not before going through a lot of soul searching and perfectionistic reform school.

When you are a perfectionist, everything drives you crazy. If you are two minutes late to a meeting, you're a wreck. You beat yourself up over burning a piece of toast or getting a stain on your favorite shirt. When everything bugs you, you end up melting down into a pile of low self-esteem. When everything is a crisis, then nothing is good enough.

Because everything bugs you, you take everything personally, and in addition to making you miserable, it can also make you depressed. You focus on failure and how to avoid it. By spending all of your energy avoiding failure, you overthink every little setback, instead of seeing each situation—good or bad—as a lesson. Wasting energy this way can make you less resilient when the big things come around.

Perfectionists are easy to spot in a crowd. They are the ones who overreact to any criticism. You may be one of those defensive souls who can dish it out but can't take it. I was like that until I met my husband, who is worse. I actually saw myself in him, and that helped me get over my perfectionism. We learned to tease each other out of our "It must be done this way" moments. In the end, I've realized that most people are very aware of their own behavior; they aren't watching your behavior as closely as you think. I used to think people were watching my every move and commenting about me. In reality, they were more worried about themselves than about me. That thought has freed me up in so many ways but has helped the most in allowing me to be myself.

Another feature of perfectionistic thinking is that you feel that you are not quite ready for "prime time". You focus on all the things you haven't accomplished, rather than acknowledge how far you've come. "If I can finally get this position at the company," you tell yourself, "then I will be happy," or "If I can just find the right person, then I can be married."

Such thoughts send you down the perfectionistic rabbit hole of overachieving and trying to reach elusive goals that may not be part of your life plan.

In fact, it is better to think the opposite: "I am happy right now, so if the right position comes my way, great; if not, that's okay." "Being married would be great, but I need to not jump in too quickly. I need to wait to find the right person." It's the opposite of what you probably grew up thinking. If you are in the right frame of mind in terms of feeling happy, doors magically open for you, and the universe often helps you achieve those goals. In the wrong frame of mind, you can feel the doors closing and the goal slipping away.

Part of getting in the right mind and out of the perfectionistic brain is being happy for the success of others. A classic perfectionist does the opposite. Have you ever been happy because someone else failed? Have you ever happily discussed that failure with your competitive and perfectionistic friends? I think you and I know that the answer is yes. In fact, as a parent, this is the hardest perfectionistic trait to get over. For a moment, just a moment, it does make you feel better. But in the long run, it is just another perfectionistic rabbit hole, one that reinforces competitive and negative thoughts.

The worst part of thinking about every little thing is that you often feel guilt, embarrassment, and shame. You are trying so hard on the outside to keep up the perfectionistic front that behind the scenes, you are crumbling. You are so concerned about the external rewards of being perfect that you forget about the feelings of being internally happy. So what is the cure for this? The cure is to be yourself and not worry about what others think. That means showing your guilty side, your vulnerable side, your embarrassing side, and your shameful side.

Brené Brown, writes about those emotions in *Daring Greatly*. Only one is bad for you, and that is shame.

"If you … say, 'I'm sorry. I made a mistake,'" Brown writes in an article for Oprah.com, "If you're experiencing guilt, the answer is yes: 'I made a mistake.' Shame, on the other hand, is 'I'm sorry. I am a mistake.' Shame doesn't just sound different than guilt; it feels different. Once we understand this distinction, guilt can even make us feel more positively about ourselves, because it points to the gap between what we did and who we are—and, thankfully, we can change what we do."

Guilt is okay. Being vulnerable is okay. Feeling shame is not okay. Guilt gets you up in the morning to go to work or to go to your kid's soccer game.

Vulnerability helps you to meet and connect with people, including your future partner in life. Shame just takes away all those things and makes you feel not good enough. So how do you get over shame? By being yourself—your unadulterated, crazy, quirky self. Let your hair down, so to speak. Let family and friends and even lovers see you as your authentic self. It's not easy at first; you may have to remind yourself to do this several times a day, but it will soon be automatic, like brushing your teeth. One of my favorite sayings is by Ziad K. Abdelnour: "I tried to be normal once ... worst two minutes of my life."[6]

6   http://www.oprah.com/spirit/
life-lessons-we-all-need-to-learn-brene-brown#ixzz4qKqA4woF

Chapter 16

Go with the Flow ━━━━━━━━

The millennials call it being chill. Zen masters call it being at one with the universe.

Nothing seems to bother you when you're in the flow. You take every situation as it comes. You don't sweat the small stuff. You are engaged.

When you are locked in, in the moment, experiencing all life has to offer, you are in the flow. You see it with athletes at the top of their game, so much in the zone that they don't even remember the game or race because they are so focused on the task at hand. So how do you get into this Zen state? The first step is to be aware. When those perfectionistic tendencies arise, and judgment and criticism are on the tip of your tongue, stop those thoughts. Then, if you can, get into a state of mindfulness, a state where everything is happening as it should be, unfolding just ahead of you. Feel the joy of that moment. Feel the flow.

I know. Easier said than done. Life is messy. It's hard to be mindful in the middle of chaos, but doing these few things will help get you to a place of peaceful, non-perfectionistic thoughts. First and foremost, breathe. As a radio newscaster, I am forced to be locked in and in the moment. Things come at me at all directions. I often describe it as being in the cockpit of an airplane during a storm. People are talking in your ear, things are moving at breakneck speed, and you have to sound calm and intelligent. I can't think about my son's upcoming meeting with the school or even what we are having for dinner. I am intensely in the moment, and in a flash, my five-hour anchoring shift is over, and I am on my way home, trying to de-stress from the fires, earthquakes, and floods of the day. The best way to do that is to just breathe.

When you focus on your breathing, in and out, stressful and otherwise negative thoughts melt away. You accept that the universe is in your favor and that by practicing mindfulness, you are being led in the right direction. You have to accept change. Change is inevitable; fighting it will only bring you fear and stress. When you slow down and watch your life unfold in front of you, allowing things to happen as they are supposed to (or not), you are in the flow. This is when your instinct comes in. The more you are in the flow, the more your intuitive mind opens up and lets you know the way to go. Your inner compass tells you the right time to act on your instincts. This type of thinking helps keep you in the present moment and be confident in your decisions.

Here are some more tips for being in the zone and going with the flow: Once you have done the breathing, focus on one thing, like the most important thing to you in the moment or something you're very interested in. Use all of your senses—taste, sight, touch, smell, hearing—to focus on the present moment. As you go through each sense, you focus on just that one thing, in that one moment, and it allows your brain to slow down and focus. Athletes often do this to get into the zone. They are able to filter out the crowd, the competition, and their nerves by zeroing in on one thing, like their breathing or by repeating a mantra to themselves over and over again.

The best way to get better at flow is to practice, practice, practice. Do this in a familiar environment so that you can filter out the excess noise and distractions. Many football coaches increase the noise level at practice to simulate a real-game situation. You can do this with almost anything. When our kids were little, we practiced trick-or-treating before they actually went out into the neighborhood (Connor was afraid of who might be at the door). This pre-event warm-up helps reduce your anxiety and allows you to get into the zone quicker and with more confidence. But remember: There is always room for mistakes; be prepared for what could happen, but believe that you are good enough.

Chapter 17

Yes and And ━━━━━━━━━━━

This is one of my favorite tricks to not letting the perfectionistic feelings overwhelm you. It works when anxiety arises, for example, in a job interview.

The first step is to say to yourself, *Yes, I am nervous or anxious about this upcoming interview.* Let yourself feel those emotions. Then continue saying to yourself, *And I will go through with the interview and perform to the best of my ability.* You can also use it in athletic performance. "Yes, I am very nervous about my race, and I will try and stay in the moment and filter out distractions." "Yes, I am scared about this test, and I am going to be ready to take it." "Yes, I am worried about this doctor's appointment, and I am going to go to the appointment and not cancel because of fear."

Just changing that one word from "and" to "but" makes a huge difference in your attitude.

"Yes, I am nervous or anxious about this upcoming interview, but I will go through it anyway."

"Yes, I am nervous about my race, but I will try."

Notice how that one word "and" makes a huge difference in the attitude of the sentence and, therefore, your attitude approaching the event. You must start your sentence with "yes" because starting it with "I don't know" or "I'm not sure" minimizes your feelings.

Who isn't at least a little nervous about a job interview, race, or test?

Chapter 18

Embarrassment

Thinking back, the fear of embarrassment was the main thing that led to my perfection problem. It could have been something as simple as wearing the wrong thing or saying something stupid. Embarrassment is different from shame, where you feel inside that you are a bad person for saying or doing the wrong thing. Embarrassment was saved for performance-based events, like a race, job interview, or test, or, if you're a parent, your child's behavior. That was a tough one for me because having a child with autism is filled with moments where he does not act like a typical child would in that same situation.

One of my most embarrassing moments was with my daughter Kasey at our neighborhood swim club. In the San Francisco Bay Area, recreational competitive swimming is a big deal. About twelve thousand kids participate in meets at private country club pools. At the end of the summer is the big county meet. Kasey was ten at the time and had made the finals in the freestyle, but her flip turn was still not great. Since I had been an All-American college swimmer, I felt I could help her, instead of counting on her coaches. One Sunday, I took her to the pool and made her practice flip turn after flip turn. She just wanted to play on the diving board, but I, the perfectionist, wasn't going to have my daughter do a bad flip turn. I pushed a little too hard, and she started crying. From the corner of my eye, I could see parents glaring at me, talking amongst themselves about me and my "tiger mom" behavior. It was a low moment in my parenting.

I helped Kasey out of the pool, and we left. I apologized in the car, and we went for ice cream; we talked it out, but I don't think she ever forgot the crazed look in my eyes. One piece of advice: If you were a competitive swimmer, don't coach your own kids in swimming. Coach them in something where you don't have a clue.

So what is an athlete, student, or parent to do about the wonderful emotion called embarrassment? One of the best techniques I have found, although it's not easy, is to simply think about something else in that moment. Swimmers wear nothing but a small piece of clothing on their bodies, so there are plenty of times they can be embarrassed. In that moment, get your mind to think of something else that has made you happy: your last vacation or your best friend. Keeping your brain from getting into that reptilian fight-or-flight mode will help to keep you relaxed and not focus on the thing you are embarrassed about.

This is important when you have to speak in public. I am on the radio a lot as a news and sports anchor: a job with a lot of potential embarrassment on a daily basis. The way I get out of my reptilian brain is by visualizing one person I am talking to directly. I visualize their face, usually a family member or friend, and I imagine that I'm only talking to them one-on-one. This is one of the main teachings in broadcasting school: A bright, upbeat, one-on-one voice delivery is the cornerstone to becoming a news reader.

So let's use this theory in practice. In a job interview, instead of thinking everyone is staring at you, think of one person (perhaps a family member, friend, or mentor) and imagine you're speaking to them, while making eye contact with the interviewers. This will keep you in that relaxed, confident state we talked about earlier. I guess those experts weren't far off when they said to imagine your audience naked.

You don't have to visualize a person; you can also think of a place, a favorite pet, or a special event that gives you the same happy feeling. Anything you feel will keep you from being anxious, worried, or embarrassed will work. But you have to hold that thought in your mind and not let the nerves back in to take over your brain.

This technique can help with social anxiety, as well. Say you are in the supermarket and run into your old boss, and it didn't end well last time you saw each other. Instead of ducking behind the bananas and hoping for the best, you decide to meet him face-to-face. Rather than going into the "This is so embarrassing" mode, red face and all, think of something happy, like for the sake of this story, your dog. Here comes the boss, right toward you, with his much-younger third wife. *Dog, dog, dog* … And boom, no embarrassing feelings, and a pleasant encounter is had by all. I often think of Hawaii when I want to stay out of the reptilian brain. Visualizing the beaches, the sunsets, the food, the Mai Tais makes me feel warm and fuzzy.

What is yours?

Chapter 19
Smith College

S mith College, a private women's liberal arts college in Massachusetts, teaches its students about failure. In fact, the administration calls it "Failing Well." Students and faculty write about their failures often, and they are printed out for everyone to see. In an article in the *New York Times* in 2017 written by Jessica Bennett, the school touts the program as a cure for what many students suffer from: depression caused by a feeling of having to be perfect. "What we're trying to teach is that failure is not a bug of learning, it's the feature," Rachel Simmons, a leadership development specialist at Smith, told Bennett. "It's not something that should be locked out of the learning experience. For many of our students—those who have had to be almost perfect to get accepted into a school like Smith—failure can be an unfamiliar experience. When it happens, it can be crippling."

Crippling. That is a good word to describe the paralyzing fear that takes over in those perfectionistic episodes we know and do not love. But I do love this professor Rachel Simmons, who herself dropped out of a top-notch school and was told she was an embarrassment. Oh, that word "embarrassment" again. In her program, according to the *Times*, the students sign a permission slip to fail. It says, "You are hereby authorized to screw up, bomb, or fail at one or more relationships, hookups, friendships, texts, exams, extracurricular or any other choices associated with college ... and still be a totally worthy, utterly excellent human."

Students put this quote on their dorm room walls. I want to send this to every college freshman that I can.

"We are talking a lot more about the advantages of failing. Failing upward," Bennett writes, is now an acceptable term, especially in the start-up community, with many tech entrepreneurs crediting failure for helping them eventually succeed in business. But the article explains that in the high-stakes academic world, many students still can't handle even minor disappointments, like getting an A minus in a class, or not getting the dorm they requested. Some of these students are so afraid to fail that they don't take any risks at all, at a time where they should be taking quite a few.

Smith is not the only college addressing this problem. Cornell,

Stanford, Penn State, along with a number of universities around the country are having to teach students life skills to deal with the disappointments in life.

So why are all these students so stressed out? Researchers say part of the reason lies in childrearing. If you grew up with a helicopter parent or are one yourself (if you'll admit it), then you basically are not prepared (or have not prepared your child) for the real world. In the "Everyone gets a trophy" world today, not many have experienced failure by the age of eighteen. And if you are the star student or athlete in high school and then are put in an environment where everyone excels, it could set you up for a perfectionistic breakdown. Colleges are increasingly finding this happening.

Students are unprepared for the demand of college; they're unprepared to get a B or to not make the travel team in their given sport.

So what to do? Kick your child when they are down, tell them that they're losers, to help them make it through the college years? Not exactly, but don't sugarcoat things. Don't make things easy for them. Do get involved if needed, especially if it's a serious issue with academics, drugs or alcohol, or mental health. If you're the one leaving for college, realize that this is the time to try and go it on your own a little. Your parents will be there if you fall, but it's okay to not involve them in the minor scrapes that often come up in college life. In the end, it's four years of dramatic growth for both student and parent, filled with failure as well as success.

Enjoy the ride.

Chapter 20

I Can't ... I'm Too Busy!

T hree college researchers recently wrote a paper about this subject.

Silvia Bellezza, marketing professor at Columbia Business School, Georgetown's Neeru Paharia, and Harvard's Anat Keinan found was that if someone seemed busy, they were viewed as more successful and held in higher esteem than those who were perceived as less busy. For perfectionists, busyness is their crack, so to speak. If you are busy enough with the perception of working hard, you set yourself up for disappointment at any minor setback that keeps you from being busy. In one experiment, the researchers used social media posts to gauge whether participants thought the posters were of high or low status. Posts that claimed "busyness" over "leisure" were perceived as higher on the status scale.

Dr. Susan Koven practices internal medicine at Massachusetts General Hospital. In a 2013 *Boston Globe* column, she wrote:

> In the past few years, I've observed an epidemic of sorts: patient after patient suffering from the same condition. The symptoms of this condition include fatigue, irritability, insomnia, anxiety, headaches, heartburn, bowel disturbances, back pain, and weight gain. There are no blood tests or X-rays diagnostic of this condition, and yet it's easy to recognize. The condition is excessive busyness.[7]

It's a sickness now. And for perfectionists, the fear of making a mistake can either paralyze you or send you into a busy frenzy to avoid what you really need to do: stay in the moment. You know what you need to do to cure a case of the busy bees. Relish every moment, taking your time to stop and smell the roses. But what if you *do* have a lot to do?

There are two kinds of busyness: the kind you can control and the kind you can't control. The busyness that is out of your control could be your job or your family. The busyness you can control often includes stress that is self-created. The over-the-top kid's birthday party, the too-many volunteer

7   http://www.huffingtonpost.com/scott-dannemiller/busy-is-a-sickness_b_6761264.html

committees you signed up for at work, or the full-kitchen remodel in the middle of having another child.

So what can you do about your busy disease? Is it a terminal? Will you have "She died because she wouldn't take a break" written on your tombstone? The good news is, no. The first step is to remember not to brag about your busyness. Try to streamline responsibilities if you can. Let go of some of the control and ask for help. Most of all, don't be afraid to make mistakes along the way. Being too busy, aside from all those physical symptoms, can wreak havoc on relationships, both personal and professional. You don't want to be in divorce court telling the judge that you ignored your partner, family, and friends to stay busy, when you had the choice to stop and smell the roses.

Chapter 21

Write It Down

W riting is therapy for me. I often go outside and sit by my pool and get so involved in words that before I know it, four hours have passed. As a reporter, I usually write short, broadcast-style sentences, so when I get a chance to just let it rip, it feels very freeing, almost Zen. I know that sounds weird, but I feel like it almost flows out of my head and into my fingers, without much in between. Whether you type it out on a computer or write longhand, putting your thoughts down on paper can be life-changing.

I'm not much into journaling, but for many people, transcribing your thoughts into words can lead you to mental clarity and health. There are many ways to go about journaling. One of my favorites involves writing down three things you are grateful for, three times a day. It could be at mealtime, after parking your car at work, or just on your phone in between meetings. Just doing this exercise three times a day can transform your life. Your gratitude can include anything, from being thankful for getting a good parking spot at work to rejoicing over finishing a project to being excited about the new salt shaker you bought for the table.

But wait; you're not done yet.

After you write down the first three things you are grateful for, also write down three goals for the day. They can be simple, like getting some errands done or setting aside time for exercise, or cerebral, like trying to stay in the moment at the post office or meditating at the end of the day. If you fail to write down your gratitude list or forget to write down your goals, don't sweat it. Try again the next day.

This exercise has been known to help perfectionists calm down and focus on what's important. Other benefits of journaling include helping you take your jumbled thoughts and put them down on paper in a clear, concise way.

You may not even realize what you're really thinking until you write it down and read it over a few times. Writing your thoughts can also help you resolve arguments or disagreements with your friends and relatives. Instead of lashing out at them, first write down the reasons why you are upset and then brainstorm ways to solve the issue. Most of the time, this action defuses the problem long enough for you to find a good solution without confrontation.

Another way journaling can help is to track your feelings and emotions over time. You can look at past patterns in your thinking and see how you solved those problems in order to unravel current issues in your life.

There is no downside to journaling (except no one writes longhand anymore, so that could be a challenge).

Chapter 22

You Are Not a Fixer-Upper —

I love that show where a couple takes the worst house in the neighborhood and turns it into the crown jewel. It's one thing to take down walls of a house. It's quite another to do that with a person. Here lies the dilemma for those who suffer from perfectionism: By comparing yourself to others, you are inherently saying there's something wrong with you. If only you could be thinner, faster, stronger, or even smarter, things would be perfect. Those "if only" statements can be dangerous because they push your thinking into the future, taking you out of the present moment.

In reality, you don't need any fixing up. Thinking of yourself as flawed is flawed thinking. You are perfectly imperfect as your unique self. Yes, you can improve on certain areas of your life, but your thoughts should not be that you are not broken. You are whole and wonderful, just the way you are.

The one place where you can be separated is in your mind. The world of Zen talks about two brains: the logical thinking brain and the abstract observing brain. The thinking brain is like the toddler who is told not to eat the cookies on the counter. All she can think about is the cookies. So trying to control the thinking brain can be difficult, at best.

Most problems happen when both brains are acting as one. Someone does something you don't like at work, for example. If both brains are on the same track, your emotions can ramp up enough to lash out at Joe for taking the last bit of coffee or at Carol for taking the last pencil from the cabinet.

What you want to do is separate out your thinking brain from your observing brain. Your observing brain would see that yes, someone is bugging you at work, but instead of thinking Joe took your coffee, say to yourself that you have the feeling that Joe took the last bit of coffee. You have the feeling that Carol took the last pencil from the cabinet. Just rephrasing how you think about things encourages your brain to observe instead of react.

One more way to get you into the observant brain is to pretend your problem is outside of you, like a television show or a movie. You are just watching the characters play out (with or without a laugh track; your choice). Think of what actors you would want to play the people you are thinking about. Then see your problem as a cartoon, perhaps with a SpongeBob or Scooby-Doo voice. This will defuse the situation, make you laugh, and eliminate the highly charged negative emotions connected to those feelings. Observing your life as a sitcom or romcom gives you the opportunity to step back from the problem and see it in a more objective way.

Lastly, laughter really can be the best medicine. I work in the news business, and we have something called "newsroom humor." It is utterly inappropriate and gross. It's probably the only way we get through a lot of the tragic stuff we have to talk about every day, but it can be so helpful in processing what is actually happening. Most of it I can't talk about publicly, but when they were electing a new pope at the Vatican, we had a pool. My engineer, Richard, who is one of the funniest people I know, made a pope hat and smoked his vape pen in the studio in response to the smoke that comes out of the chimney when they have picked a new pope. Then there is the usual death pool, where we pick which famous person is going to kick the bucket next. I know, it's pretty gross, but if you've ever worked in a newsroom (or an emergency room, for that matter), that is how they deal with what life throws them.

If you can laugh at yourself and others in a healthy way, you'll be able to take the bumps and bruises of life in stride. If I only knew this in high school, when I fretted over everything

I said and did. I look back on those times now and wonder why those things mattered so much. I could have used these techniques to defuse a number of situations that I handled poorly. I should have asked myself, would this situation or person matter next month, next year, or in five years?

Probably not.

Chapter 23

So What Would You Do if You Were Good Enough?

O kay. So let's say you read all the chapters of this book and you are thinking this Kim woman is onto something. You started the book with Steph Curry and Tom Brady. Those two guys are onto something. The next few chapters, we delved into the perfectionistic myth. The quicker you learn to fail and fail well and forward, the better off you will be. You realize that giving 90 percent is way better than 100 percent and that laughter truly is the best medicine. Let's see how your life will be after reading this book.

You will live in the present moment. You will show up in your life and watch it unfold in a magical way. You will trust your feelings that things will show up at just the right time, along with the right people. You will live in a state of gratitude, thankful for the little things that make your life more enjoyable. You will feel a sense of freedom to do and be anything you want to be. You will see yourself as whole, not a broken person in need of fixing. You will feel imperfectly perfect in every way. You will embrace failure as a necessary learning tool and welcome challenging things that take you out of your comfort zone. You will be fearless in your efforts because either way, you learn a lesson.

You will know that when you come from a place of love, anything is possible.